*Legend
of the
Walled-Up
Wife*

Ileana Mălăncioiu

LEGEND *of the*
WALLED-UP
WIFE

Translated from the Romanian
by Eiléan Ní Chuilleanáin

Wake Forest University Press

First American edition published 2012

For permission, write to
Wake Forest University Press
Post Office Box 7333
Winston-Salem, NC 27109
WFUPRESS@WFU.EDU

Printed on acid-free, recycled paper
in the United States of America.

Library of Congress Number 2012943150

ISBN 978-1-930630-61-1 (paperback)

Designed by and set in Arno Pro
by Nathan W. Moehlmann,
Goosepen Studio & Press.

Wake Forest University Press
WWW.WFU.EDU/WFUPRESS

Rugă

Pe regele Oedip îl ducea de mînă fiica sa Antigona,
Pe Regele Lear, Cordelia, cea alungată
Din împărăția lui că nu l-ar fi iubit îndeajuns,
Pe tine aș putea să te duc eu, tată ...

Prayer

King Oedipus had his daughter Antigone to lead him by the hand,
King Lear had his Cordelia that he banished
Out of his kingdom for not loving him enough,
And you, father, I would be able to lead you ...

from Rugă, on page 62

Contents

Translator's Preface

ILEANA MĂLĂNCIOIU WAS BORN in 1940 in a village near Câmpulung in Argeş, about 100 miles from Bucharest. She trained originally as an accountant but began to write poetry, took degrees in philosophy (her doctoral dissertation was on 'tragic guilt') and worked in journalism and films.

From *Păsărea Tăiată* (*The Slaughtered Fowl*, 1967) onward, her poems draw on rural life and folklore, on religious and literary icons, but their true focus has been on the trauma of history. In an early poem, 'Bear's Blood', translated here, the peasant remedy is juxtaposed with actual state violence: the man addressed as Ieronim had suffered terrible injuries as a political prisoner. Ten more books of poems appeared in the 1970s and '80s, and in 1992 came the full text of *Urcarea Muntelui* (*Climbing the Mountain*, 1985) which had been heavily censored by the Ceauşescu regime. Newer poems have been included in two recent enlarged collections spanning her whole career to date.

The selection of Mălăncioiu's poems in this book is based on two collections published in Ireland, *After the Raising of Lazarus* (Southword Editions 2005) and *Legend of the Walled-Up Wife* (The Gallery Press 2011). Some poems which were included in the earlier volumes have been revised. This edition also contains the Romanian originals of four poems, 'Bear's Blood', 'Prayer', 'Legend of the Walled-Up Wife' (in the original just 'Legend'; the legend is well known and has many variants in Eastern Europe), and 'In My Steaming Mirror'; they offer samples of her early, middle, and late work.

Mălăncioiu's writing is valued in Romania as a moral force. A courageous critic of the former political masters of her country, she has also been forthright in her responses to the new order. To read through the poems published under Ceauşescu is to be astonished both at what she succeeded in publishing, and at her survival. Censors and secret police may not have been the most penetrating readers of poetry, and in fact her major clash with the regime was on her attempt in 1988, when she was editor of the literary review *Viața Românească*, to publish work by the controversial philosopher Constantin Noica, another former political prisoner. The issue of the magazine was suppressed and she resigned. If it had appeared, that issue would also have contained her poem 'I Could Have Come', translated here, a good example of her dense, tense blend of oblique Biblical reference and direct questioning of a culture of collusion.

Writers under censorship can employ many strategies; personae from Melville's Ishmael to Yorick to Antigone, metaphors from folklore, the Old Testament and Orthodox Christian ritual, all can be deployed without being devalued or reneged. A ruse is her repeated attaching the title 'Pastel' to poems expressing prophetic or personal rage. It is borrowed from the delicate, plaintively autumnal and rural poems of George Bacovia (1881–1957), and there are allusions to her rural background in the poems so labelled. However they assert anger and frustration — she characteristically describes her own voice as a shout or scream — framed and almost stifled in seasonal lyric.

Another of her repeated titles is 'Rugă' which can mean 'prayer' or merely 'request' in Romanian; I have used each term once for the two examples in this selection, as the context and tone seemed to demand. In general, my translation is as faithful to Mălăncioiu's words as possible, given that I also wished to reflect the colloquial fluency of her poems by offering versions which might be consonant with an ordinary Irish speaking voice. The casualty has often been rhyme, so much harder to manage in English than in a Romance language.

Legend
of the
Walled-Up
Wife

A Request

I'm asking you, fearless lad,
Though you climbed the wall of death at the children's fair,
Don't come to rescue me from the seven-headed giant
In hopes of half the kingdom for your reward.

I came to this place of my own free will,
I swept the cobwebs from the hearth,
I kneaded the earth twice over and
I filled all the ovens with bread.

Then I broke it roughly in a cloth,
To let out the heat, and he felt it far away,
And instead of a thrown club a humming like a storm,
A great sniff from his fourteen nostrils.

I waited for him to find out the taste of the bread
And only after a bump of my heart I found all was well,
He was buried in the earth up to his breast
And from the shoulders up jammed in the moon.

Come all you girls who belong in this story
You have been stalked so long by dread,
When it is so simple and so human
Just for once to try falling for a giant!

Custom

After seven years the dead are disinterred,
The bones laid side by side in boxes,
And even if the forehead bone is eaten away
They are mourned like people living and whole.

Three days they remain in the holy place
Flowers are brought and placed at their head and feet
They are told about who has been born,
They are given charge of the people who are dying.

And then our heads begin to ache
With all the lilies around them, and turn by turn
We move away from the blue flames,
Chanting for their return into the earth.

The gravediggers ready at the head and feet
At the proper moment come together
To leave them back in the graves they had before
And lay on top of them a firmer stone.

Ieronim Sleeping

He sleeps with his head on my arms
With open eyes, it is late,
And I am afraid to take my arms from under his head
It's quiet and I lean against him.

You have one glass eye, Ieronim,
A little bluer than the other
A little rounder too a little deeper
And it has ridges on it like the old glass icons.

In the middle is a hole like a pupil
And it seems to bear a trace of weeping and it is
So cold that I begin to shiver:
Ieronim I'm afraid, wake up Ieronim.

But he stays there with his head on my arms
And he sleeps with open eyes and he dreams
That he will never wake and I cry out to you all:
Quiet, please, quiet, Ieronim is sleeping.

A Night Almost Sleepless

That night I hardly slept (Lord, what a night it was!),
I was gazing at Ieronim and his body was lit up
Right to the bones. Mr Ieronim, I cried,
(For at that time I called him Mr Ieronim)

Please pardon me for what I say, I'm frightened,
Sir, your body is now no more
Than a vague shape of light and through it
I can see plainly all the broken bones.

For I tell you, in that night, right through his body
They were quite visible, all his broken bones
Down to the stooped bone of his forehead
And silver gleamed from its side.

That was a night I could not sleep, Lord, what a night it was
And how afraid I was alone with Ieronim
And his body shone so brightly that
Through it appeared every one of his broken bones.

The Water of the Dead

Today I roved out through the fields, Ieronim,
And saw for the first time the waters of the dead
And I ran over to them and in their midst
I saw you stripped for bathing.

It seemed you wished to cover yourself and somebody
Had stolen your clothes from the bank
And as I came closer to you
You fled ashamed taking the waters with you.

And I was sorry you ran away, Ieronim,
Since I presumed that you had fled for shame
For in that water where you moved
Great scars were visible on your body

And I saw the scars and I ran off and followed
The waters of the dead across the fields . . .
What a fine looking man you were, Ieronim,
And how I feared that I would not catch you!

Sînge de urs

Ca să te vindec, Ieronim, ți-adusesem
Sînge de urs, în șoaptă te rugam:
„Gustă puțin, îți va face bine,"
Și întru adevăr, credeam că în noaptea aceea
Cu sînge de urs te-aș putea vindeca.

De sînge tu nu te-ai putut atinge,
Cu sila am vrut să ți-l torn pe gît,
Vîscos era, deasupra buzelor rămînea,
Îl dezlipeam încet și-l aruncam
Și cu altă cană de sînge veneam.

Dinadins îl vărsai și strigai către mine
Și nu știi, Ieronim, cît de rău îmi părea,
Altfel aș fi vrut să fie în noaptea aceea chiar dacă
Oasele tale zdrobite, în grabă la loc adunate,
Sîngele de urs să le vindece nu mai putea.

Bear's Blood

To make you well, Ieronim, I had brought you
Bear's blood and I begged you in a whisper:
'Just taste a little, it will do you good.'
And truly I believed that in that night
With bear's blood I could make you well again.

You couldn't stand to touch the blood.
I tried to pour it down your throat by force,
It was so thick it stuck to your lips,
I unstuck it gently and threw it away
And came again with another cup of blood.

You deliberately spilled it and screamed at me
And you don't know, Ieronim, how sorry I was,
I would have wished all otherwise that night, although
Your crushed bones, piled hastily together,
Even the blood of a bear could not hope to heal.

Over Against the Mountain

The heart of the queen has risen up out of the rock.
Only I in silence come
To the place where she was buried
To pay respect to the hollow that remains.

Over against the mountain is the cross,
The inscription now rewritten by the wind,
A white lily hides the place
Where it enters the earth.

The night gets darker still,
Silently I circle the gates
With the royal arms, closed
Between me and the hollow place.

The Heart of the Queen

Natanael, I think the rats are moving through the citadel,
The royal bed — look, it's been eaten away,
Out of the rock in their overnight raid
They have carried off the heart of the queen.

The people come and they want to know
Where is the heart of her majesty the queen,
It is hidden away in his press,
The watcher has gone mad with shame.

Natanael, be on your guard,
The city will be destroyed:
Set neat poison out from place
To place inside the walls.

I think the rats are moving through the citadel,
Stone by stone they are taking it apart
Natanael, the queen's heart is gone out of the rock
And I am ashamed and I am full of fear.

Hush, Bride, Don't Weep

Let's drink the wedding wine, the bridegroom
Is dead, and the bride as well,
All the guests are dead and in the earth I hear
How the wedding dance spins around.

Hush, bride, never shed a tear,
Your mild bridegroom is here,
Like a lamb his eye fills with sleep,
Like a lily he shines in his dream.

He only pretends he is made of stone,
Hush, bride, do not weep, do not fear,
Over your eye like a wedding veil
There grows a crust of ice.

Maybe It Isn't Him

I've found your body stabbed from behind,
It would have been much harder otherwise,
I pull the blade out terrified and wipe
Its gold handle on my breast and side.

Lord, I cry, maybe it isn't him,
Maybe it's only his earthen shape,
Maybe the blood is not actual blood,
His soul maybe is singing across the plain.

Maybe the birds are listening to his song,
And that's why over the plain they are all
Silent, maybe they too are made of clay
And their only use is magical.

Maybe it is death barely now arrived
That hunts the mystery of the sacred being
After whose form we were contrived,
Maybe the eternal bird is singing.

It Snowed on the Body

Snow fell fine in the mountains towards the peaks
We seemed the first to walk through the harsh season
When we found a trail of blood in the snow
And then the body where it was leading

Was lost we almost thought there was nothing
Lost too the trace that brought us to the spot
Only the blood thickening sharp on snow
Pressed quickly through the thin dazzling white

We stared astonished how the trace reappeared
Constantly from somewhere among the mountains below
The snow fell on the body before our eyes
It fell slow on the crows stripping the bones

Pastel

Fresh air and the smell of digging around the vines
And the fruit trees white by the gates
We are back again in spring, with the same
Dreams and some deaths to mourn

We bury the seed deeper
To protect it from birds and from frost
The graves have sunk, new leaves are sprouting,
Perhaps their souls have made it to the sky

I bend over grass springing from the clay
That sinks in the levelling rain
Everything seems as it has always been
Only one grave still does not sink away

The air is chilly, the wind blows around,
The souls seem to have faded into the cold
I see not one certain sign of the life
Of the one whose loss makes me cry aloud

The Call Has Been Answered

The call has been answered, this sun
Has risen over the green field.
The soul unfolding as a snail
Slides out of his enclosing shield

He dawdles across the long empty
Space it seems he drowns
In light he flourishes over the white wave
Two melting jellied horns

He feels no gravity at all,
He has come all the way out as in a dream
He strolls he seems turning to go home
But the shell is closed to him

Song of Joy

Coupled with my guardian angel
We were only couples boarding the ark
And we lived through the curse and we came ashore
In that ancient country
Where the people placed their wishes
In the entrails of birds
And in the land as seeds.

There you brought me secretly sparrow's eggs
For my meal in the morning
And cuckoo's milk in the evening
And joy for all my life
And one intense grief
Because it could not last
Until old age.

All passed in great secrecy
We woke and the quince had flowered overnight
The sparrows never knew when you stole their eggs
We did not know the hawks had hatched their brood
On the roof of our house, we rejoiced
In the land where we had come ashore
And the sky under which we waited.

She Came into My Chamber

She came into my chamber in the darkness
Holding two knives in her hands
Like two brilliant mackerel
Pointed by their own will towards
The body of the one destined to die.

She was wearing transparent gloves
Reaching up to her elbows,
She changed the knives from one hand to the other
Making as if to sharpen them
But seemed to say: I cannot.

Well, I cried out, rebellious,
Neither can I,
Only I understand
That I have been permitted
To make a choice.

But she still gazed at that certain
Spot placed on my back
And at the mackerel which had suddenly forgotten
How to swim so terrified that if I could
I'd have done the whole job myself.

Like a White Bird

Like a white bird his soul sits in the palm of my hand,
What seed should I search for, what song should I call,
What fire has struck him down, Lord, in this silence
From his path to heaven?

He came with his wings trailing,
With fear and sadness I halted beside him,
He seemed to have eyes all over his body
Like your cherubim appearing to Ezekiel.

About us I saw the cloud in which he came
And his four faces unseen
And the four wheels of chrysolite
That brought him where you commanded.

He told him to stay in my hands, I said to myself,
In his wheel is the spirit which brought him here,
Lord, do not punish those who catch souls like birds,
When you call him he will arise.

You Were a Cross, Eagle

Eagle, you were a cross, and you had
His body on you for three days
And you had eyes on wings and on claws
And nails in your eyeballs.

To you I prayed weeping,
To the spirit that carries him off
To the cross of his wings,
To the cross.

It remained empty before me
Its wood rotten like a body,
I listened to the wind battering
And the broken pieces falling.

Give Me a Sign

One long night a black spider
Catching in his wide spreading web
My free flight, my sleepwalker's ramble
Towards the roofs covered with snow.

You silently regard my vertical
Even small-stepping pace
And my trembling hands like antennae
That finger the universal fear.

Give me a sign to interrupt me,
In the depth of the dream I start to confound
Day with night and right with left
And the walls upon which I climb.

The Monument

We were building a huge funeral monument
Like nothing ever raised under the sky
It had to be as wide as the whole townland
And as high

To see it we raised our eyes with dread
From the great chain-
Gang where we shifted stones from side to side
And back again.

We were building a huge funeral monument
It was almost done to the best modern plan,
Some last bits and pieces still needed doing
And it definitely needed a dead man.

The Fool

Someone was looking at my head
As Hamlet looked at Yorick's skull,
It's the fool's head he said
And I regretted the way I made the king laugh
When my body was twisted up with pain.

I regretted that even Hamlet in his grief
Remembered only the laugh I raised
And he was able to rise
Out of the grave and to gaze
Into my empty sockets

As he might look in the eyes of Ophelia
After the water carried her away
Seven years later and more
Or as he'd look at his old father
Or at himself

In a moment of supreme madness
When laughter and weeping are all one.
I did not know why he had given the word
For the kings to take my head in their hands and gaze
With pity, as they might look at the fool.

There Are

There are dark halls, there are butterflies
Clinging to cold corners,
There are bedchambers with mildewed walls,
There are snakes lying on the paths,

There are dogs that bark at midnight,
There are hours of agony and eyes that never close,
There are nights when imagining a huge spider
I see it in truth hung from the wall

And I wallop it and forget I've knocked it down,
There are boomings and sobbings and whispers,
There are mornings when I look in astonishment
At the corpse of the little insect I killed in the night.

As I Was Travelling

When I was travelling as an obscure
Member of Ahab's crew
Searching for the white whale
Suddenly I felt my right leg
Shedding its flesh and becoming
A plain artificial stump
Whittled from the sacred bone
Of the Leviathan.

Captain Ahab, I called out
No louder, no more softly,
Than I needed to be heard
In the boom of the ocean
Through which we slid one behind the other
Propelled by the warm current
Of my soul.

Don't you see how even yet unharmed
The same dreadful accident carries us on
Towards the monster who sank his fangs
In you at sea
In me in my purest dream
Where everything was repeated
With even more intensity and pain.

Captain Ahab, I begged,
But there was no sound only silence,
The ship had left me behind
It fled on with incredible speed
While I searched alone for the white whale
Somewhere on the opposite side.

Doubtless you'll say the fear
Of the great voyage is nothing
Compared with the great voyage itself
But I say it all weighs on my shoulders
Since I took the place of the ship and the waters
And of the crew which accepted my madness
And of the whale that swallowed us down.

One More Hour

One more hour and I would have seen again
The sun racing above the clouds
And how it flared and fluttered at the edge
As at the early dawn
Of another life. One more hour
And I'd have looked again on the narrow valley where I lay
And counted the pine-trees pointing at the horizon
And the birds above me as I dreamed
And the ants that walked over me
As if on their own sad weary way.
One more hour and I would have felt them stinging
And rejoiced that I existed
And rejoiced that I was other
Than this howling silence.
One more hour and that black cloud
Would have moved away from the sun.

Game

I take my share of pebbles
And pile them in the riskiest way
And I start to play, convinced
That anyway I will lose.

Why are you playing, then,
You will ask me.

What else can I do,
I will answer.

Then silently
I will continue moving
Stone after stone,
Mountain after mountain.

Cheerful Songs

What cheerful songs they sang
Those ten women in the hospital
On the Sunday of Shrovetide,
What a carnival

The masks clinging to their thin cheeks
And what a voice you had when you said:
You see, I'm keeping my word, I don't weep,
You see, I've given up being sad.

So sadness was gone even
When death began to cut down
Somebody every day
You all went on singing party pieces

In a terribly natural way
And all the world shook with the happy sounds
From that narrow dark ward
In the Mercy Hospital.

My Sister as Empress

My sister is in her kingdom;
She was in a huff with us here
She took her crowns and went away
But mother and father believe
That she will reappear.

She'll surely be back, says father,
How could she leave
For her heavenly kingdom
With slippers on her feet?

But mother with womanly feeling
Feels that her girl can't come
With a crown on her head, in slippers,
In broad day, back home.

She'll come at night, says mother,
Father says in the morning,
I alone know my sister has gone for good,
Won't be returning.

I saw the place where she passed
Hidden under seven
Crowns so her parents would not know
And I followed the trace of her slippers
To that other kingdom in heaven.

You Have Not Absolutely Left

You have not utterly gone, not utterly
Gone. My brain in fever holds you
In its most secret inner cell
Where you are well again.

You know where you are, though you pretend
To know nothing any longer, fed to the teeth
With all that's past, you think all the time
Of how to escape from this cell.

Your hands with unreal grace
Secretly dig grey caves
All the watchmen of the world guard against your escape
But who can stand in your way?

Last night you got away for a few instants,
I saw you clearly as you came out of the flame
How you trod lightly over my left temple
And went back willingly to your place.

You Gave Me a Long Look

You looked at me long and distrustfully,
Why haven't you done your eyes today, you said
Once, and said it a second time
And the woman in the next bed said
Go on, Miss, make-up your eyes.

So I went shaking to the mirror
Where your bed, reflected, appeared
Gently sloping, as if
You and the bed were sliding down
And I began

To do my eyes up, slowly, slowly,
As if I were doing a sum
So as not to cry out in pain
And calmly you said to me
You're much better like that.

The Doctor on Duty

Go quickly, she said to me, I'm afraid,
You see that Dr X is on duty,
He surely knows what to give me to help me to breathe,
He told me nobody dies while he's on the ward.

And indeed, that very young doctor
Who was not as famous as his heart was good
Came in the middle of the night and gave her
Something that kept her breathing until the next day.

After that she understood
That his shift was finished and we had entered
That terrible day which already
She had started to say she would never get through.

The one who was on duty looked down
On us without interfering:
I never said that nobody dies
While I am on duty, I am not at fault.

I Thought It Would Be Just You

I expected it to be just you,
There were three dead bodies in a cubicle,
Death dragged itself through the damp cold
Like a shining caterpillar.

A young man standing by
Wept extravagantly
More than he had to weep
And kissed you insanely.

You loathed being lamented and kissed
And we felt the greater grief, since
You seemed to have always been there
While we had just happened along.

And we didn't know what to do,
Luckily you knew how to behave,
You stayed smiling and calm
In between those other dead.

Then I Understood

Then I understood, you were alone
In the grey dead underground
And I myself beside you
As at the world's other end.

The priest sang the usual office,
The acolytes murmured their lines,
I saw how the earth fell on you
And wondered how I didn't die.

Father wept, but went on living,
Mother's tears were dry,
Your children had not yet learned to weep,
The wind didn't know what it blew.

It rocked the wooden cross that told
You were not yet thirty-three
When you left us, gently as it rocks
A grove of flowering trees.

I remember well, you were alone
In the grey dead underground
And I myself beside you
As at the world's other end.

They Were at the Table

There they were at that same table
You had lain on for three days,
They were more ravenous than ever
But nobody had the courage
To lay a hand on you, to break into
Your sweet fragrant flesh.

They started with the soul,
Said I to myself, that must be the custom,
Looking now at you,
Now at the mouths wide opened
To drink that holy drink
Which foamed up

When it was swallowed
There at that table
Without fear
Without any thought of ill;
Take, eat, I woke up shouting,
This is her body!

In Forty Days

In forty years I did not learn
As much as I learned in those forty days
When I had no need
Of any teaching at all.

All I needed to know was how to walk
To the very end and let myself go
Into the life that comes after this
As from the edge of a precipice.

I walked from morning until evening
And I thought of how you no longer know
Even how to walk and how you must learn
Only in those same forty days

What the others have learned
In forty million years
When they had no need
Of any teaching at all.

The Spider

In the morning the spider comes out of the dark
With his long delicate legs
And wanders a while in the bed
Where I receive news of you.

But I thought I caught you yesterday morning, say I.
But I thought you were even more horrible,
But I thought I was afraid of you
But I seem to remember I slaughtered you.

It wasn't me, he tries to explain,
Look closely at my leg how it breaks
And my intact body where there isn't
Any least trace of blood.

Apart from the fact I know you, I whisper to him
Spiders never bring anything but bad news,
And he tells me that if I let him off
I will see in the night again your soul

Suspended somewhere above
Since last spring
When it was forced out of the fragrant flesh
As from its own homeland.

But I can't stand it any longer, I cry,
And in terror I squash him on the tiles
And the next day quietly strolling
Across my temple, there he is again.

From the Cold Frosts of Autumn

From the cold frosts of autumn
You rose like a light haze
You floated in the blue sky
Like cloud changing its shape.

At first you were a little girl
Bent over her own image
As if she could see no otherwise,
As if she played in the sand.

Slowly, slowly you grew
And looked down on the doings below
Fearfully, sadly,
It all seemed lovely to you.

Presently you joined with another cloud
You both watched the flight of the birds
And how the cloud-children grow in the sky
Then you merged with the other clouds.

I Came to Her House

I was at her door, I knocked,
I heard her soft voice muffled
Her steps on the far side of the stone wall
And I called out that I had come.

Who are you she asked, who are you looking for,
I know nothing of the time or place we were happy,
My sisters are those girls who died
At almost thirty-three.

Don't you remember me, I demanded,
I brought you anemones and baked potatoes,
I stayed at your bedside faithfully
Seven days and seven nights.

You died in my arms I was going to say,
But there was nobody to speak or to hear,
She had opened the door and then I saw
Nobody dies in anyone else's arms.

Laid Beside You

Lying beside you
In the grandparents' burial plot
Where you can see right into the church
As far as the altar
I waited for the priest to come out with Holy Communion.

The people were dressed up as in the old days,
They knelt with their backs to us,
Nobody knew I was buried,
If they had called to me I would have answered
From under the flat stone

Which I had pulled over me slowly
Without knowing
As I might pull a blanket
Where we were sleeping together
Leaving you half bare.

I looked fearfully at the altar,
Not knowing why the Communion was not brought out
And I fretted when nobody came,
Then by good luck you felt the bitter cold
And pulled away the stone slab covering me.

Dream and Reality

The pine-tree in front of my house
Was as high as the mountain,
The cells that grew random in your hip
Were like a concentration

Camp. In that monstrous place
You commanded, interned alone
Without pity or compassion
You placed in the centre a bone

It was set up like a gallows
For the hanging of your flesh,
You were the pine-tree in front of the mountain
And up you climbed in a flash

Yourself the Roman soldiers on guard
For your agony throwing dice
Your bruised body like a seamless
Garment was their prize.

A Mountain Feeling

Warm sun and the airs of spring,
Snow lingering only on the peaks,
We imagine them with longing,
But who now climbs the mountain to go there?

Cliffs shine in the blue distance,
Beside them everything seems petty,
How can you have a sense of the mountain
When you too are a mountain now?

The mountains know nothing of their own greatness,
Their name is so often taken in vain,
Some people have gone mad and think they are mountains
But who can tell them the terrible truth?

In My Brain

In my brain is the mountain I used to hope,
Overthrown, brought low, buried,
Everything would fit, and I could take it with me
In the day when I set forth.

What is in your brain, I was asked,
I stayed calm, a mountain I answered,
And they took me away, mountain and all,
I was silent I placed my trust in the shining cliffs.

But they took out the mountain stone by stone,
And they looked again inside my freshly shorn head
As into a totally transparent egg
And there they found even more hidden things.

A Calm Inviting Sky

A sky calm, inviting,
The mountain rises really to the sky,
Whoever could climb the mountain on this day
Would enter into the terrible mystery

As into his own garden
And would perish like the seed
To bring forth fruit tenfold
But who can climb the mountain now?

All has been sold off already,
All is in order, all quiet.
The chalice that should have been drained is now
A lavabo for governor Pilate.

Somewhere in Transylvania

Somewhere in Transylvania in an old church,
I saw a saint who carried his skin on his back
And the skin kept the shape of the body where it had been
And the saint kept his faith from days that were gone.

That could be seen by the light from his forehead
And by his hollow ribs which seemed to cause him no pain
And the fact that the skin looked so like him
And did not seem to be all that light to carry.

Somewhere in Transylvania in an old church,
I saw a single body that was prepared to die,
He carried his soul on his back in his own skin
As he might have carried a precious load.

The Horse

In a pitch-dark night when I was all alone
In the narrow corridor of that hospital thinking
How could they never have discovered the right pill
Just then I heard the sound of a horse's hooves.

I had no notion how to stop the sound,
In fear I descended the stairs
And in the cold air of night
I felt the horse's muzzle cool and damp.

But he began to climb slowly,
Moving like an ancient man
Dragging painfully his worn hooves
And the fragile traces of hay

Which shone through the bare ribs
Outlined, as if picked out in gold
And I watched him as he opened the door
And as he swallowed down

The flowers of camomile on the bedside table.
Enough, he said, you don't need these,
And then he neighed as he used to do
And passed between those two curtains.

It was our horse dead the year before
She was gazing after him and I didn't know what to say
I thought again how could it be possible
They had never discovered any cure at all.

Legendă

Stau într-un zid ca Ana lui Manole,
Numai că eu nu sînt Ana, iar cel care m-a zidit
N-a visat nimic niciodată.

El m-a închis într-un zid gata făcut,
În propriul său zid de apărare,
Ca să nu fiu nici înăuntrul hotarelor lui,
Nici în afară.

El visează abia acum la sfîrşit
Şi umblă să mă scoată din piatră seacă,
Dar nu mai ştie unde m-a zidit.

Legend of the Walled-Up Wife

I am inside a wall like Manole's wife Ana
Only that I am not Ana, and the one who walled me in
Has never had a dream in his life.

He enclosed me in a wall ready made,
In his own defensive wall
So that I would be neither inside his boundary
Nor outside.

He dreams only now at last
And moves to release me from the dry stone,
But he no longer knows where he walled me in.

Just That

I had fallen asleep wearing a shift of skin,
Said they, that is forbidden by the rules,
And they hauled me into a sitting position
And pulled it easily off me.

I wasn't surprised they stripped me bare without asking,
They had their obligations to think of,
What amazed me was the way my thin skin
Could so easily be peeled away.

It remained all in one piece
A shift of plain stuff,
If I'd had a bit of light I could
Have stitched embroidery on it.

Just that it had got turned the wrong way around
And I couldn't turn it the right way again,
Just that nobody had thought
To put a needle and thread under my pillow.

Beginning the End

Silence, the beginning of the end,
A deep grave is digging slowly, slowly,
And from time to time earth falls on one
Who is smothered and dies.

All the people scrabble with their nails
After the body of one buried alive,
Who never even thought of death,
Digging slowly into ash-grey clay.

He dug long, it is later related,
Dug at his grave meant for the boss himself
And just then the earth collapsed
On his own bent shoulders.

Nobody was near, the others were digging too
In another place, a deep, deep grave
They dig slowly, slowly and from time to time
On somebody the earth falls.

A Crime

A crime committed on the principal street
At high noon, a dreadful crime,
And nobody cries out, nobody screams,
Nobody grabs the criminal.

I am there myself writing poetry
As if my poems might stop
A crime done on the principal street
In broad daylight.

Oh when will I put everything aside
Go out into the street and shout as loud as I can:
A crime has taken place, arrest the criminal,
I am an accomplice, arrest me too.

Rugă

Pe regele Oedip îl ducea de mînă fiica sa Antigona,
Pe Regele Lear, Cordelia, cea alungată
Din împărăţia lui că nu l-ar fi iubit îndeajuns,
Pe tine aş putea să te duc eu, tată,

Pe mine nu ştiu dacă se va găsi cineva
Să mă-nsoţească-n momentul acela oribil
În care ochiului meu i se va ascunde totul,
Pe noi toţi ştiu bine că va fi imposibil

O, Doamne, nu orbi tot neamul meu deodată,
Ia-ne din doi în doi şi mai amînă
Sfîrşitul tragediei, lasă-i la fiecare
Pe cineva să-l ducă-ncet de mînă.

Prayer

King Oedipus had his daughter Antigone to lead him by the hand,
King Lear had his Cordelia that he banished
Out of his kingdom for not loving him enough,
And you, father, I would be able to lead you,

But for myself I do not know if one will be found
To bear me company in the dreadful time
When everything will be hidden from my eyes,
I know it will not be possible for us all

O Lord, do not blind all of my people at once,
Allow us to go two by two, postpone
The last scene of the tragedy, let each one
Lead one other slowly by the hand.

We've Had Snow

We have had snow, a blizzard, we've had the lot,
There's nothing more to come from the sky,
Nor on this earth, however hopefully
You've been watching that window's frosty white.

Come away, don't hope any more, don't
Stay longer with your nose stuck to that glass,
It has gone, youth too has gone, the frozen
Winters are no more we used to pass

Gliding slowly from one age to the next,
From one life to another, from one hell
More terrifying than Hell itself
There where souls fall

As if naturally, without caring
As snowflakes fall upon a cross
As the eye of the dying falls
On the last thing that is lost.

Calm

Yet one more carries a cross on his back
Calmly as he would carry a sack to the mill
And we all follow as he enters the graveyard
And nobody shudders at all

To see he has written his own name on a stone
Which he intends to mark the green ground,
He has just paid for as if he were afraid
That as the other one has disappeared

His would be quickly lost. One more
Who moves quite calmly there
To his own place, the cross he carries on his back
He has been learning all his life to bear.

In Memoriam Virgil Mazilescu

It rains and now Virgil starts to drink water
And theorizes that water is not so bad.
He knows quite well what drink this is,
And how often he will have to drink it.

And yet he made haste to get hold of his ration,
Perhaps because he's thirstier than us,
Perhaps seeing how every thing passes he feared
That in the future it might not even rain in the ditches,

Perhaps he chose the exact moment he'd waited for,
Perhaps at last he is cooling down,
And as in drink shouts all that comes in his mind
Or maybe he is silent there as a fish

Without anyone forcing him, and is proud
As nobody ever has been before
That he has only ritually poured down
His throat the ditch-water that is our portion.

Quiet

Quiet, a single explosion in a cellar,
A single voice indignant in a public square
A single butcher found slaughtered
In the market hall one morning

A single radiant incendiary fire,
A single sadness muffled,
A single shadow without end
Cast over all life and lifeless things.

A single way of falling,
A single way of salvation
We wait for it to drop from heaven
On one great day.

Random Thoughts

Random thoughts, written in the dead of night
On this table where I shred green herbs
And the meat of rabbits
And whatever else can be shredded,

In the place where, at the same time as, in the machinery
Which spins all the slow heavy day
In my night shelter, in the kitchen
That I painted myself

White, aseptic, anachronous,
And yet very, very much what's needed
If you ever again have anything to say
And haven't got into the way of writing in the larder

Or in the lift or so, in general
Indifferent to all the jumble
In which the one who does the shredding is mixed
With what gets shredded

Day by day the same sauce and those
Vital flavourings which substitute,
While I stay at the table and I tremble
And still write verses and do not know why.

Antigone

A frozen hill, a white dead body
Left above ground fallen in the hard fight,
Starving dogs come to tear at the traitor snow
And another winter comes and tears it too.

Let a maiden appear, let her tread down the commandment,
Let her drag that imaginary hill away from the dogs
And hide it as if it were a dear brother
At the same time as you all wash your hands

And you will let her go living into
The tomb that's robed in that unreal white
As in the time when the Emperor lost the great
Battle she mourned and gave burial to a hill.

Two Friends

It snows and once again covers the traces
Of this saddest winter of all
Snowing on those who have gone so it seems
They need never have been here at all.

I want to get out of here, who knows
How many winters I can face,
I pull this graveyard on to my back
While still it snows and I leave.

Two friends call softly out of the snow
Dear one, you can't bring us along, not so,
You are not permitted to carry more
Than one cross when you go.

Pastel

Springtime, now every ailment is rampant,
If anyone is to die it will be now,
If it is not yet blooming
Father's grave will soon burst into flower.

Mother has set flowers of every kind
Just so the time would somehow pass by,
While I am budding again with an idea
That will cost me dear.

Just now I can't follow it up
A spring breeze strikes up its mourning tune
With ominous words, of a woman
Who went mad in wintertime.

I Could Have Come

I could have come along with you to supper
Forgetting the betrayal that was to be,
But I saw you were all on the watch,
You knew what the price was, you couldn't tell
Who was going to be sold and who would sell.

Now when the betrayal comes about
Of all the actors in the show
Only Pilate plays his part,
Washing his hands, although he knows
Christ himself is absent from the great mystery
And a sinner has taken his place in history.

Confounded you look at Judas
Who has taken the silver pieces and run away
While the sinner who was sold has been forgotten
His crucified body starting to decay.

The Dead Are No Good at Games

The dead are no good to play with,
They are too sedate, too solemn,
They take existence far too seriously
They are too in control of their destiny.

They are too poor to lose anything
Compared to us, to the living,
They can't sell themselves for anything in the world
You can't pay your debts with them,

You can't do anything with them
They can't be sentenced
Nor even lifted up from the earth,
How could you make them sell themselves

Again, for a more comfortable place?
On that old stairway definitively climbed
They have paid all that could be paid
For the equality they have received.

Pastel

It is spring, I am in a flowering meadow
Rejoicing that I am free, that I can
Be here, like a countryman
Buried in his own garden, house and all.

I place on paper a hard thought to accept
With the illusion that I am still alive;
A worm danders along as if through a corpse
Through the pages of my notebook as I write.

Return

We had returned, nothing was as now,
Without wishing to I had fallen asleep
And begun alone to test myself
As if the Lord had been testing me.

Father was still alive, we worked that hard
Earth of ours with its poor enough harvest
And I brought you an offering of the grain
And hoped you would be happy to accept it.

And yet I knew father was long dead
And I had brought that offering for him,
When I suddenly noticed your nostrils quivering
Hankering for the smell of roast lamb.

We had returned to the old times, far in the past
Were '48 and the Tower of Babel
And the smell of lamb roasting made me afraid
For our brother Abel.

Again in the Deserted Square

Again in the empty square where I stood and wept
With other despairs and other dreams
There with the same decaying cross
That awaits us too with open arms.

Let us approach it bringing bread and wine
Nothing has changed even the same dismay
And the starving dead more and more wearily
Devour the wreaths left on the commemoration day.

I Look into Your Soul

I look into your soul broken free of your body
And in the depth of night entering my room,
Sad, exhausted, alone,
Not accustomed to walk without its garments

Its flesh and its bones, not accustomed
To a gaze that goes straight to the inside,
It sits down before me and it shines
And shivers like a lamb.

I release it into the darkness
And it floats on the water
And returns to the body
Which fits it no longer.

Fulcrum

I was dead, but I could still get about
Over land and water and another dead woman
Walked below envying me
And began to drag me down.

I swam impeded through the thickening waters
Slackly dragging her towards that other shore,
Just as she dragged at me on her side
And we held on expecting victory or defeat.

I was dead, but I was still able to get around
And that dead woman held on to me,
With all her strength as I held on to her,
Searching for a fixed point to take my weight.

From the Bluish-Green Sky

The tree in the middle of the field begins to bud,
From the bluish-green sky come angels and saints,
Mary mother of God still young and beautiful
Watches them, they are so well-behaved.

Where is the time when St George
Knew it was his task to defeat the dragon,
Where is the time when the Angel of the Lord
Would have been able to take the bull

By the horns, even if he knew all beforehand?
There is a quiet that bodes no good,
Luckily one with decomposing flesh has come forth
Out of the grave dug on purpose under the plum-tree

So we wouldn't forget the place. Luckily one came forth
Out of his grey grave into the world;
With an even deeper odour of death
We have all entered into spring,

Only one, two, three, four, five
Climbed up into the isolated tree
Stuck in the heart of that graveyard
And they look down on me from the sky.

În oglinda mea aburită

Totul a fost pregătit, moartea își spală părul
Și îl piaptănă în oglinda mea aburită
Din care argintul începe să curgă,
Cineva cască gura să îl înghită

Dar nu reușește, cineva cască gura
În care lumea ar putea să încapă
Cu imaginea ei cu tot și mi-e frică
Să intru din nou în această apă

Tocmai acum, cînd moartea își spală părul
Și îl desparte printr-o cărare dreaptă
Care taie în două tigva ei asimetrică
Și oglinda în care m-așteaptă.

In My Steaming Mirror

Everything has been readied, Death washes her hair
And combs it in my steamed-up looking-glass
The silver on it begins to run,
Someone opens engulfing jaws

But doesn't succeed, someone opens
Jaws that could fit the whole world and then
Her image on top, and I fear
Entering into that water again

Just now, while Death washes her hair
Divides it in two makes the parting straight
Slicing in two her asymmetrical skull
And the mirror which is where she waits.

Back, to the Promised Land

From time to time your cry gets past the gravestone above me,
I feel it because of the vibration of the green moss
Grown there between the rotten autumn that's past
And the spring when hope begins to germinate.

I walk hours together in this flowering graveyard,
I am free to walk as much as I can, I am free
To die right here on the spot or between
Those four walls of mine where I have waited

For the Annunciation. Indeed I am free, Lord, I say to myself
While I walk around just like one who was dead
Fresh risen out of the grave, who doesn't know
What to do next. Fortunately time passes anyway

Whether I run all day like an ant,
Whether I feed myself with manna from heaven,
While in fear I cross this desolation
Going back, to the promised land.

Confession

Life was sweet to me as the shore is sweet
To the sailor when at last he comes to land
After a long voyage over the sea.

Hard for me to learn to look out for danger,
And how to walk on the land as if on water.
What consoled me was my father defending

The family spot in the graveyard there
Where there is no room for even one more grave,
And that above my life there is another.

I obeyed and I succeeded, father teach me
How to live among the dead of the family,
Teach me how to be alive among the dead.

I No Longer Dream of Flying

I no longer dream that I fly, no longer dream
That I'm hanging on to the edge of the roof,
I don't fall from high places, don't wake in the night,
Father, my sleep resembles yours,

My sleep resembles death even more closely,
But if death is like sleep, then
I can take courage while you stretch out
Your hand whose fingers are worn thin by rain,

Until I wake or until again the Angel
Comes close and stops me falling from the edge
Where I hang until His hand comes to stop the Angel
Who is ready, ready to fall for the second time.

History Repeats Itself

The story repeats itself, Jesus carried his cross
As Isaac bore the bundles of firewood
Piled on his shoulders by his old man Abraham
Only your son could not be substituted

As his was, with a ram prepared for sacrifice.
Concerning the much-trumpeted resurrection of the dead
Nobody mentions a word, but they've understood
Instinctively that it is getting near.

Their almost imperceptible movement
Makes me shiver on my legs,
A live current scatters the heavy air,
Who are you, brother, how have you risen

Beyond the nature of these and of those others.
Your cold breath has frozen our hearts,
Forgive us this day our new daily fear
Forgive us our new Fear.

After the Raising of Lazarus

De mortuis nothing but good, of those arisen
A fortiori more good. But I can't stop myself wondering
What has become of Lazarus, the one after the raising of Lazarus
Whose traces have been lost as if
He had never existed and what am I
After you took me out of my silence, sister of death?
For how much time, for whom and for what
Did you raise me up? On this earth there is nothing more
On which I can truly found my trust,
In heaven nothing to be made out. After
The gravestone was moved aside and you called me
Until I emerged from my grey grave,
Although I was bound hand and foot,
So that my trace may not be entirely lost
On the road I travelled once
To the end, with your infinite power
Over me, return me to my own death.

Acknowledgments

THANKS ARE DUE to Ileana Mălăncioiu for her hospitality, and for giving up her time to discuss the poems; to Raluca Rădulescu who originally taught me Romanian and advised on the 2005 collection; and to Diana Nacu who came to talk Romanian to me in my office in Trinity, and advised on the later poems. Thanks also to Cormac Ó Cuilleanáin and Macdara Woods who read and advised on drafts of some or all of the translations.

A number of these poems appeared first in *After the Raising of Lazarus* (Southword Editions, Cork, 2005) and in *Legend of the Walled-Up Wife* (Gallery Press, Oldcastle, Co. Meath, 2011). Thanks are due to the publishers, Pat Cotter and Peter Fallon.

Some of these poems (or versions of them in Irish) appeared in *Cyphers* and *The Stinging Fly*.

The original versions of these poems were published in Romania in a collected edition, *Urcarea Muntelui* (Editura Corint, Bucharest, 2007).